THE
QUESTION of
FORGIVENESS

THE
QUESTION OF
FORGIVENESS

Brian Zahnd

Charisma
HOUSE
A STRANG COMPANY

THE QUESTION OF FORGIVENESS by Brian Zahnd
Published by Charisma House
A Strang Company
600 Rinehart Road
Lake Mary, Florida 32746
www.strangbookgroup.com

a division of Good News Publishers. Used by permission.

Cover design by Justin Evans
Design Director: Bill Johnson

Visit the author's website at http://brianzahnd. com.

Library of Congress Cataloging in Publication Data:
An application to register this book for cataloging has been submitted to the Library of Congress.

International Standard Book Number: 978-1-61638-372-5

E-book ISBN: 978-1-61638-416-6

11 12 13 14 15 — 987654321
Printed in the United States of America

CONTENTS

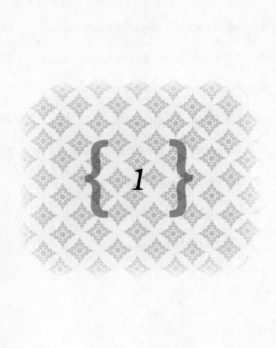

{ *1* }

FORGIVENESS . . . ALWAYS?

I T SHOULD BE obvious that forgiveness lies at the heart of the Christian faith, for at its most crucial moments the gracious melody of forgiveness is heard as the recurring theme of Christianity. Consider the prevalence of forgiveness in Christianity's moments of birth and sacred texts: As Jesus teaches his disciples to pray, they are instructed to say, "Forgive us our sins, for we ourselves forgive everyone who is indebted to us."* As Jesus hangs upon the cross, we hear him pray—almost unbelievably—"Father, forgive them."† In his first resurrection appearance to his disciples, Jesus says, "If you forgive the sins of any, they are forgiven."‡ In the Apostles' Creed we are taught to confess, "I believe in the forgiveness of sins."

Whether we look to the Lord's Prayer or Jesus's death upon the cross or his resurrection or the great creeds of the church, we are never far from the theme of forgiveness—for if Christianity isn't about forgiveness, it's about nothing at all. Whatever else may be said about Christian people, it must be said of us that we are a people who believe in the forgiveness of sins—we believe in the forgiveness of sins as surely as we believe in the death and resurrection of Jesus Christ. Most of us enter the Christian faith at least somewhat motivated, if not primarily moti-

---

* Luke 11:4
† Luke 23:34
‡ John 20:23

vated, to find forgiveness for our own sins. As we grow in the Christian faith, it is vital we become aware that we are called to be those who extend forgiveness to others, thus making the world a more forgiving place. If we enter the Christian faith to find forgiveness, we must continue in the faith to become forgiving people, because to be an authentic follower of Christ we must embrace the centrality of forgiveness.

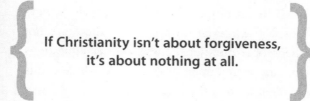

If Christianity isn't about forgiveness, it's about nothing at all.

That's the theory anyway.

But in the real world of murder, rape, child abuse, genocide, and horrible atrocities, how viable is forgiveness? Is forgiveness just a pious idea that can flourish inside stained-glass sanctuaries, only to wither in the harsh realities of a secular world where stained glass cannot hide the ugliness of human atrocity? A rape victim may have learned the Lord's Prayer as a child in Sunday school, but does the part about forgiving those who trespass against us have any bearing upon her situation? Is she supposed to forgive her rapist? Sure, forgiveness is good in the realm of relatively minor transgressions, but is there a limit to forgiveness? Are there some crimes that go beyond the capacity of forgiveness? Are there some sins so heinous that to forgive them would itself be an immoral act? Is forgiveness always possible? Or even always right? These are not theoretical questions; these are real questions that are forced upon us in a world where evil is so often beyond the pale.

For modern people, the iconic image of evil and the leading candidate for the unforgivable is the Holocaust and the evil architect of that atrocity, Adolf Hitler. Indeed, the Holocaust casts a long shadow over many aspects of the Christian faith and challenges Christian validity on several levels. While considering the topic of forgiveness, we must ask: Does the Christian concept of forgiveness have anything to do with the Holocaust, or is genocide indeed the realm of the unforgivable? When Christianity speaks of forgiveness, should there be an asterisk attached to the word to indicate that forgiveness is not applicable in extreme situations like the concentration camps of Nazi Germany, the ethnic cleansing in the former Yugoslavia, and the tribal massacres of Rwanda?

I've had people tell me not to worry about these extreme cases, because to teach people to forgive one another in the ordinary course of life is enough. But I disagree. If it can be shown that there are situations in which the call of Christ to love our enemies and forgive our transgressors does not apply, we have found the loophole to escape any meaningful Christian obligation to forgive others. Forgiveness then indeed becomes merely an ideal of piety restricted to a stained-glass showcase. The questions about how far forgiveness can and should extend are real questions asked by real people—perhaps most notably by Simon Wiesenthal.

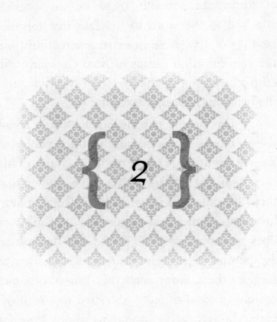

{ 2 }

THE STORY OF SIMON WIESENTHAL

SIMON WIESENTHAL HAS a haunting story to tell, and an even more haunting question to ask. He tells his story and asks his question in his famous book *The Sunflower*. Simon Wiesenthal was an Austrian Jew imprisoned in a Nazi concentration camp during World War II. In *The Sunflower*, Simon Wiesenthal tells his story and then asks the reader a hard question.

As the book opens, Wiesenthal is part of a work detail being taken from the concentration camp to do cleanup work in a makeshift field hospital near the Eastern Front. As they are marched from the prison camp to the hospital, they come across a cemetery for German soldiers. On each grave is a sunflower. Wiesenthal writes:

> I envied the dead soldiers. Each had a sunflower to connect him with the living world, and butterflies to visit his grave. For me there would be no sunflower. I would be buried in a mass grave, where corpses would be piled on top of me. No sunflower would ever bring light into my darkness, and no butterflies would dance above my dreadful tomb.[1]

While working at the field hospital, a German nurse orders Wiesenthal to follow her. He is taken into a room where a lone SS soldier lay dying. The SS soldier is a twenty-one-year-old German from Stuttgart named Karl Seidl. Karl has asked the nurse to "bring him a Jew." Karl has been mortally wounded in battle and now wants to make his dying confession—and he wants to make it to a Jew. The SS man is wrapped in bandages covering his entire face, with only holes for his mouth, nose, and ears. For the next several hours, Simon sits alone in silence with Karl as the dying SS soldier tells his story. Karl was an only child from a Christian home. His parents had raised him in the church and had not been supporters of the Nazi party and Hitler's rise to power. But at fifteen, against his parents' wishes, Karl joined the Hitler Youth. At eighteen Karl joined the infamous SS troops.

Now as Karl is dying, he wants to confess the atrocities he has witnessed and in which he, as a Nazi SS soldier, has participated. Most horrifying is his account of being part of a group of SS soldiers sent to round up Jews in the city of Dnepropetrovsk. Three hundred Jews—men, women, children, and infants—were gathered and driven with whips into a small three-story house. The house was set on fire, and Karl recounted what happened to his confessor in these words:

> "We heard screams and saw the flames eat their way from floor to floor.... We had our rifles ready to shoot down anyone who tried to escape from that blazing hell.... The screams from that house were horrible.... Behind the windows of the second floor, I saw a man with a small child in his arms. His clothes were alight. By his side stood a woman, doubtless the mother of the child. With his free hand the man covered the child's eyes...then he jumped into the street. Seconds later the mother followed. Then from the other windows fell burning bodies...We shot...Oh God!"[2]

Karl is most haunted by the boy he shot, a boy with "dark eyes" who Karl guessed was about six years old. Karl's description of this boy reminds Simon Wiesenthal of a boy he knew in the Lemberg Ghetto.

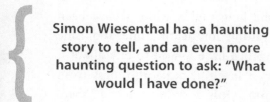

Simon Wiesenthal has a haunting story to tell, and an even more haunting question to ask: "What would I have done?"

During the several hours that Simon the Jew sat with Karl the Nazi, Simon never spoke. At Karl's request, Simon held the dying man's hand. Simon brushed away the flies and gave Karl a drink of water, but he never spoke. During the long ordeal, Simon never doubted Karl's sincerity or that he was truly sorry for his crimes. Simon said that the way Karl spoke was proof enough of his repentance. At last Karl said:

"I am left here with my guilt. In the last hours of my life you are here with me. I do not know who you are, I only know that you are a Jew and that is enough.... I know that what I have told you is terrible. In the long nights while I have been waiting for death, time and time again I have longed to talk about it to a Jew and beg forgiveness from him. Only I didn't know if there were any Jews left.... I know that what I am asking is almost too much for you, but without your answer I cannot die in peace."[3]

With that, Simon Wiesenthal made up his mind and left the room in silence. During all the hours that Simon Wiesenthal had sat with Karl, Simon never uttered a word. That night Karl Seidl died. Karl left his possessions to Simon, but Simon refused them. Against all odds, Simon Wiesenthal survived the Holocaust. Eighty-nine members of his family did not. But Simon Wiesenthal could not forget Karl Seidl. After the war Simon visited Karl's mother to check out Karl's story. It was just as Karl had said. Karl's mother assured Simon that her son was "a good boy" and could never have done anything bad. Again, this time out of kindness, Simon remained silent. Simon believed that in his boyhood, Karl might indeed have been "a good boy." But Simon also concluded that a graceless period of his life had turned him into a murderer.

Simon Wiesenthal concludes his riveting and haunting story with an equally riveting and haunting question addressed to the reader.

> Ought I to have forgiven him?... Was my silence at the bedside of the dying Nazi right or wrong? This is a profound moral question that challenges the conscience of the reader of this episode, just as much as it once challenged my heart and mind.... The crux of the matter is,

of course, the question of forgiveness. Forgetting is something that time alone takes care of, but forgiveness is an act of volition, and only the sufferer is qualified to make the decision. You, who have just read this sad and tragic episode in my life, can mentally change places with me and ask yourself the crucial question, "What would I have done?"[4]

{ *3* }

IS FORGIVENESS
ALWAYS POSSIBLE?

AND THUS WE are faced with a dramatic challenge to the possibilities of forgiveness. Is forgiveness always possible? Are there some situations in which forgiveness is impossible? Is this one of them? Can a dying, apparently repentant Nazi find forgiveness for his sins? Can a dying SS soldier who participated in Holocaust atrocities find forgiveness from God? And perhaps more challengingly, can he find forgiveness from his fellow humans? Would it even be permissible to offer forgiveness in this case, or would it be a betrayal of justice? These are the kind of questions that are raised by Simon Wiesenthal's *The Sunflower*.

The second part of *The Sunflower* is a symposium of fifty-three prominent thinkers—Jews, Christians, atheists, philosophers, professors, rabbis, ministers, and others—who respond to Wiesenthal's question. The respondents understood the real question as this: Is there a way that a person in Simon Wiesenthal's position could offer forgiveness of some kind to the dying Nazi? By my count, twenty-eight of the respondents said no, offering forgiveness in this situation is not possible. Sixteen of the respondents said yes, there was some way in which forgiveness could have been offered. Nine of the respondents were unclear on their positions. Interestingly, the sixteen who were in favor of some form of forgiveness were all Christians or Buddhists (thirteen Christians and three Buddhists). Among Jews, Muslims, and atheists who responded there appeared to be unanimity in agreeing that an offer of forgiveness in this situation was impossible.

Conversely, most of the Christian respondents said there was a way in which forgiveness could be offered. Significantly, no Christian stated that forgiveness in this situation would be categorically impossible. It can't help but be noted that a Christian worldview apparently radically influences how a person approaches the possibilities of forgiveness. And it should be stressed that forgiveness here does not mean pardon in a legal sense. Had Karl Seidl lived, he still would have been subject to the demands of legal justice despite any offer of personal forgiveness. Forgiveness here should be understood not as legal pardon but an invitation back into the human community.

After surviving the Holocaust and publishing *The Sunflower* in 1969, Simon Wiesenthal went on to live a noble and humanitarian life. He died in 2005 at the age of ninety-six. In *The Sunflower*,

Mr. Wiesenthal does a masterful job telling his story, and his question about the possibilities of forgiveness is important for all human beings, but supremely so for Christians, because forgiveness is at the heart of the Christian faith.

On the cover of my copy of *The Sunflower* is this question: "You are a prisoner in a concentration camp. A dying Nazi soldier asks you for forgiveness. What should you do?" I felt it was important that I try to compose an answer. So even though Simon Wiesenthal never personally asked me his question, here is my unsolicited reply:

> Dear Mr. Wiesenthal,
>
> First of all let me say I will not presume to sit in judgment of your actions. You showed kindness to a dying Nazi soldier as you held his hand, brushed away the flies, and gave him water to drink. You showed great kindness to his mother in not destroying the memory of

her son. And I agree with Lutheran theologian Martin Marty who says, "Non-Jews and perhaps especially Christians should not give advice about the Holocaust experience to its heirs for the next two thousand years. And then we shall have nothing to say. Cheap instant advice from a Christian would trivialize the lives and deaths of millions." Nevertheless, since you ask the question, let me try to reply. I cannot say what I would have done, only what I could hope I would have done. As a Christian I would hope that I would reply in something of this manner to my dying enemy:

"I cannot offer you forgiveness on behalf of those who have suffered monstrous crimes at your hands and the hands of those with whom you willingly aligned yourself; I have no right to speak on their behalf. But what I can tell you is that forgiveness is possible. There is a way for you to be reconciled with God, whose image you have defiled, and there is a way for you to be restored to the human race, from which you have fallen. There is a way because the One who never committed a crime cried from the cross saying, 'Father, forgive them, for they know not what they do.' Because I believe in the death, burial, and resurrection of Jesus Christ, I believe that your sin does not have to be a dead end, that there is a way forward into reconciliation.

"The forgiveness of which I speak is not a cheap forgiveness. It is not cheap because it was not cheap for Jesus Christ to suffer the violence of the cross and offer no retaliation but love and forgiveness. It is not a cheap forgiveness because it requires of you deep repentance, including a commitment to restorative justice for those you have wronged. There is no cheap forgiveness for your sins, but there is a costly forgiveness. If you in truth turn from your sins in sorrow and look to Christ in faith, there is forgiveness—a costly forgiveness that can reconcile you to God and restore you to the human race. I cannot forgive you on behalf of others, but on my own behalf and in the name of Jesus Christ, I tell you, your sins are forgiven you. Welcome to the forgiving community of forgiven sinners. May the peace of Jesus Christ be with you."

This is what I hope I would have said. But for all I know, I might have treated a dying enemy with far less kindness than you did.

IN DEEP ADMIRATION
OF YOUR DIGNITY,
BRIAN ZAHND

As I read the responses from the twenty-eight or so who argued against the possibility of offering forgiveness to the dying Nazi, I found many of their arguments very compelling. Nevertheless, I'm convinced that if forgiveness is impossible for a repentant war criminal simply because his sins are too terrible, then the Christian gospel is a fairy tale, and we might as well abandon the charade. But as the Apostles' Creed says, "I believe in the forgiveness of sins." Christianity is a faith of forgiveness.

- The Christian life is a prayer of forgiveness: "Forgive us as we forgive them."
- The Christian life is a suffering cry of forgiveness: "Father, forgive them."
- The Christian life is a commission to forgive: "If you forgive anyone, they are forgiven."

So even in the face of Simon Wiesenthal's challenging question and the sympathy I may feel for those who argue that forgiveness could not be offered by a Jew to a dying Nazi, I am fully convinced that to deny the possibility of forgiveness is to deny the very heart of the Christian gospel. The oft-quoted words of Jesus, "with God all things are possible,"* not only include forgiveness but also especially pertain to forgiveness. And the call of Christ to take up our cross and follow him is very specifically a call to love our enemies and end the cycle of revenge by responding with forgiveness.

> I'm convinced that if forgiveness is impossible for a repentant war criminal simply because his sins are too terrible, then the Christian gospel is a fairy tale, and we might as well abandon the charade.

---

* Matthew 19:26

Of course there is a cheap forgiveness that is worthless and an affront to justice. Essentially, the Buddhist position is that evil is a nonexistent illusion, so there is really nothing to forgive. This is nothing like the Christian position. Christian forgiveness is not a cheap denial of the reality of evil or the trite sloganeering of "forgive and forget." That may suffice for minor personal affronts, but it is hollow and even insulting when applied to crimes like murder, rape, and genocide. No, Christian forgiveness is not cheap. Rather it is costly because it flows from the cross—the place where injustice and forgiveness meet in a violent collision. Christian forgiveness does not call us to forget. Christian forgiveness allows us to remember but calls us to end the cycle of revenge.

FORGIVENESS—THE HEART
OF THE CHRISTIAN GOSPEL

I HAVE FOUND IT very interesting to ask non-Christians what Jesus taught. Nearly without exception they will mention that Jesus taught us to love our enemies. Among nonbelievers, Jesus seems to be famous for teaching that his disciples should love their enemies. Yet when I ask Christians what Jesus taught, they very rarely bring up this commandment. But I think the intuition of the non-Christian is correct—Jesus's emphasis on loving enemies is central to Jesus's teaching and is especially prominent in the Sermon on the Mount. The command to love your enemy is memorable because it is radical. But the command to love your enemy is a command that we who are followers of Christ tend to *forget* because it is so very hard to do.

Yet Sermon on the Mount Christianity is the very kind of Christianity that can change the world. The Christlike love that absorbs the blow and responds with forgiveness is the only real hope this world has for real change. To respond to hate with hate enshrines the status quo and only guarantees that hate will win—it's what keeps the world as it is. We tend to think that our hatred of our enemies is justified because we can point to their obvious crimes, and, as the logic goes, if we were in charge instead of our enemies, things would be different. But history tells a different story. Hatred, no matter how justifiable, simply fuels the endless cycle of revenge. Nothing really changes except that lines on a map get redrawn. Meet the new boss; same as the old boss. Christianity has more to offer the world than recycled revenge.

September 11, 2001, is testament to the power of hate. On that day, nineteen men filled with hate and armed with box cutters changed the world. Think about that.

- Nineteen men
- Box cutters
- Hate
- Changed the world

It seems almost incredible, but it seems to be true.

Yet as followers of Jesus Christ, we are called to believe in the radical proposition that love is more powerful than hate. We are called to believe that although hatred may be very powerful, it's love that never fails, and that love is the greatest thing of all. If we hate our enemies because they first hated us, and return hate for hate because that's what hate does, we will continue to live in the ugly world of hate and its endless cycle of revenge. But when love enters the world of hate and is willing to love even its enemies, a new and real kind of change comes to the world—a change where hate does not have the last word. Yes, nineteen men full of hate and armed with box cutters changed the world. Or did they? Did the world change, or was that day simply the addition of the latest chapter in the long legacy of hate? Maybe the world didn't change at all; maybe it's just the same old thing that's been happening since Cain killed Abel.

Jesus Christ taught us to love our enemies and to pray for those who abuse us. And he modeled it to the extreme. He carried his cross to Calvary and there forgave his enemies. As Christians, we believe that Calvary is the time and place that the world began to change. Did nineteen men full of hate and armed with box cutters change the world? What about twelve men full of love and armed with forgiveness?

Yes, in the Upper Room on the evening of the Resurrection, Jesus breathed upon his disciples and said, "Receive the Holy Spirit. If you forgive the sins of any, they are forgiven."* Loving and forgiving our enemies, this is how we are to change the world!

> **Sermon on the Mount Christianity is the very kind of Christianity that can change the world. The Christlike love that absorbs the blow and responds with forgiveness is the only real hope this world has for real change.**

During the Armenian Genocide of 1915–1917, one and a half million Armenians were murdered by Ottoman Turks, and millions more were raped, brutalized, and forcibly deported. From the Armenian Genocide comes a famous story of a Turkish army officer who led a raid upon the home of an Armenian family. The parents were killed, and their daughters

---

* John 20:22–23

raped. The girls were then given to the soldiers. The officer kept the oldest daughter for himself. Eventually this girl was able to escape and later trained to become a nurse. In an ironic twist of fate, she found herself working in a ward for wounded Turkish army officers. One night by the dim glow of a lantern, she saw among her patients the face of the man who had murdered her parents and so horribly abused her sisters and herself. Without exceptional nursing he would die. And that is what the Armenian nurse gave—exceptional care. As the officer began to recover, a doctor pointed to the nurse and told the officer, "If it weren't for this woman, you would be dead."

The officer looked at the nurse and asked, "Have we met?"

"Yes," she replied.

After a long silence the officer asked, "Why didn't you kill me?"

The Armenian Christian replied, "I am a follower of him who said, 'Love your enemies.'"[1]

She simply said, "I am a follower of him who

said, 'Love your enemies.'" For this Christian, no further explanation was necessary. For her, forgiveness was not an option; it was a requirement. Do we carry the same conviction? Do we see the practice of forgiveness as synonymous with being a Christian? When grappling with the question of forgiveness, we eventually have to grapple with the question of what it means to be a follower of Jesus. It's all too easy to reduce being a Christian to a conferred status—the result of having "accepted Jesus as your personal Savior." But that kind of minimalist approach is a gross distortion of what the earliest followers of Jesus understood being a Christian to mean. The original Christians didn't merely (or even primarily) see themselves as those who had received a "get out of hell free" card from Jesus but as followers, students, learners, and disciples of the one whom they called Master and Teacher. Jesus was the master, and they were the disciples.

{ *5* }

FORGIVENESS—THE COST OF DISCIPLESHIP

WHAT DOES IT mean to be a disciple? If someone were a disciple of the sitar master Ravi Shankar, it would be assumed that they hoped to learn to play the sitar with great skill. If someone were a disciple of a kung fu master, it would be assumed that they hope to eventually master the art of kung fu. So, if we call ourselves disciples of Jesus, what is it we are trying to learn? What is it that

Jesus offers to teach us when we heed the call to follow him? What is Jesus the master of, which we seek to learn? The answer is "Life." Jesus is the master of living well, living rightly, living truly. Jesus is the master of living a human life as God intended. And at the center of Jesus's teaching on how we should live is the recurring theme of love and forgiveness.

For those who are serious about being a disciple of Jesus, serious about learning to live the way he taught, the Sermon on the Mount is of supreme importance. This is where Jesus sets forth his radical vision of how we should live. And make no mistake about it; it is radical—so radical that for much of Christian history, the church has occupied theologians in finding ways to get around it. Some theologians have suggested that Jesus never actually expected us to live the Sermon on the Mount; rather it was a disingenuous teaching to "drive us to grace." As the argument goes, in attempting to live the Sermon on the Mount we would find it simply can't be done, and then we would look to grace as an alternative to obeying Christ. Not grace to live the Sermon on the Mount, but grace *not* to live it.

This interpretation is pretty far-fetched, to say the least, but surprisingly common. Other theologians have argued that the Sermon on the Mount should be viewed as attitudes of the heart, but not as commandments to be actually obeyed. So that as long as you have the attitude of love in your heart, you don't have to actually go the second mile or actually turn the other cheek. I suppose this means that when you are treated unkindly you can retaliate like everyone else, but you are to do so with a "kindly attitude" in your heart. Of course this turns Christianity into nothing more than a nice religion of private piety—something that has been regularly done throughout the centuries. But we should keep in mind that Jesus was not crucified for teaching people to have a cheerful attitude. Jesus was crucified for teaching there was another way to live than adhering to the pharisaical religion of Israel or the brutal empire of Rome. It should be obvious from an honest reading of the Gospels that Jesus expected his disciples to master the lessons he taught and actually live a life centered on love and forgiveness. And Jesus expects his modern-day followers to do the same—to become disciples of love who master the art of forgiveness. Jesus was under no illusion that this is an easy life. In his sermon he called it a narrow and difficult road, but he also called it the road that leads to life.

The most common and vigorous protest against any serious attempt to live the Sermon on the Mount is that it's not "practical."

> It should be obvious from an honest reading of the Gospels that Jesus expected his disciples to master the lessons he taught and actually live a life centered on love and forgiveness.

Not practical?

Practical is a very utilitarian (and at times

ugly) word. In this case, it is code for complicity with the status quo and accepting the world *as is* as the only legitimate vision for humanity. Before we can even try to live the Sermon on the Mount, we must first experience the liberation of our imagination. If we only listen to the "practical" men who run the world as it is, we will end up settling for the anemic interpretation that the Sermon on the Mount is about private attitudes of the heart and not about Jesus's radical vision of love and forgiveness.

We must keep in mind that we are told the Sermon on the Mount is not practical by those who have a deep commitment to (and perhaps a vested interest in) perpetuating the status quo. These practical men seek to control not only the way the world is run but even our imaginations. They tell us, "This is just the way the real world works," and thus they seek to confine Jesus to a "heavenly" kingdom while they get on with the practical business of running the "real" world. But the Holy Spirit is a liberator of imagination, and we must reject the arrogant pretense of the principalities and powers along with their bloody pragmatism. The church with a Christ-inspired vision and a Holy Spirit–liberated imagination is to be that realm where the followers of Jesus prove the practical men wrong by actually living the Sermon on the Mount. To live the Sermon on the Mount, we first have to rebel against the powers that be. We have to believe that there is another way of being human. We have to believe that Jesus taught and modeled that way.

> The church with a Christ-inspired vision and a Holy Spirit–liberated imagination is to be that realm where the followers of Jesus prove the practical men wrong by actually living the Sermon on the Mount.

The twentieth century was one of the bloodiest and most hate-filled centuries in human history. It was a century defined by war, especially the two great World Wars—The War to End All Wars…and the one that came after that. As the children who were born at the close of World War II came of age, they began to imagine an alternative to the hate and war that had defined their parents' generation, and so they sang and spoke of "love and peace." The problem was that no one could actually live it. As Larry Norman wryly observed, "Beatles said all you need is love, and then they broke up."[1] The "love and peace" generation of the sixties wasn't wrong in trying to imagine something better than a world filled with hate and war—it was wrong in not finding a better messiah than the Beatles. Jesus didn't just talk about love and peace; *he lived it to the extreme.* When Jesus prayed for his enemies to be forgiven as they drove the nails into his hands, he was living his own sermon and validating his right to preach it. After that, no one could dare claim that Jesus's teaching was not "practical." Jesus had lived it, died for it, and been vindicated by God in resurrection. His call is as vibrant and exciting today as it was two thousand years ago when he first issued it to Galilean fishermen:

"Follow me." It's an invitation to follow Jesus in his radical way of enemy-love and costly forgiveness.

If the only way of responding to the evil of injustice is retaliation and revenge, we conspire with the powers of darkness to keep the world an ugly place. This is why Jesus (upon his own authority!) dared to countermand the Torah and alter the law of "an eye for an eye and a tooth for a tooth" with his radical command not to resist the one who is evil and to turn the other cheek. A world in which tit-for-tat retaliation is the rule remains an ugly place where too many people are missing an eye and a tooth. Or, as Mahatma Gandhi observed, "An eye for an eye makes the whole world blind." Jesus's vision is to end the ugliness of revenge and make the world beautiful through grace.

{ 6 }

IS GRACE MORE THAN
JUST THE NAME OF A GIRL?

GRACE IS THE distinctly Christian alternative to the tired system of retaliation that perpetuates pain and leaves the whole world blind. Grace is God's idea of how the world can be made new. Grace is why Jesus could call the poor and persecuted...the mournful and meek...blessed. Jesus's entire life and message were the embodiment of the grace that triumphs over the cold

pragmatism of a world where the strong domi-
nate the weak. Jesus's message of love and
forgiveness is not rooted in a naïve optimism
but in the grace that takes the blame, covers the
shame, and removes the stain and the endless
cycle of revenge.

Grace is the antidote for the Eastern concept
of karma. Karma is the ancient idea that what
goes around comes around, and there is no
escape from it, that retribution always has the
final word. But grace travels outside the rules
of karma and gives a different final word. Of
course, the very basis of the Christian gospel is
that, because of what Christ accomplished on
the cross, there is a way for sinners to be saved
from the destructive consequences (karma) of
their sins. But Christians are not just recipi-
ents of forgiving grace; we are also called to be
those who extend the grace of forgiveness to
others. Christians are to be carriers of grace in
a world cursed with karma and endless cycles
of revenge.

> Jesus's message of love and
> forgiveness is not rooted in a naïve
> optimism but in the grace that takes
> the blame, covers the shame, and
> removes the stain and the endless
> cycle of revenge.

Grace is the great treasure of the kingdom of God, or as Jesus described it in his parable, a pearl of great price. That pearl is the gospel of the kingdom of heaven. It's the pearl of the gospel of grace that makes beauty out of ugly things. That's what grace does. Karma doesn't have the final word, and the ugliness of vengeance is not the final mark left upon humanity. What could be more ugly than the murder and rape of a helpless Armenian family at the hands of Turkish soldiers? Yet from that ugly episode emerges a beautiful story of grace and forgiveness.

So, ultimately, for the committed Christ follower, the question of forgiveness is not a question of whether forgiveness is possible, but a question of how we can find the grace to offer forgiveness. We may discover that we offer forgiveness to transgressors and offenders the same way that Jesus did—amidst great suffering. In our feelings-oriented culture, it's easy to equate forgiveness with having certain feelings. Forgiveness is not a feeling. Forgiveness is a choice to end the cycle of revenge and leave justice in the hands of God. Very often we forgive our enemies by entering into the sufferings of Christ who forgave from the cross. As Dietrich Bonhoeffer says in *The Cost of Discipleship*, "The call to follow Christ always means a call to share the work of forgiving men their sins. Forgiveness is the Christlike suffering which it is the Christian's duty to bear."[1] Dietrich Bonhoeffer was no starry-eyed idealist who didn't know about the reality of evil. He wrote these words during the rise of Nazism in Germany and would eventually die at the hands of the Nazis. Bonhoeffer's theology of forgiveness was forged in the crucible of real and costly suffering, but for Bonhoeffer, the cost of discipleship settled the question of forgiveness.

FORGIVENESS PRAYER

Forgiveness is a cyclical phenomenon and is reciprocal in nature. We forgive because we are forgiven, and we are forgiven because we forgive. Forgiveness is a divine vortex that brings all concerned to the focal point of grace where mercy triumphs over judgment. We place ourselves in a position to receive the grace of forgiveness when we adopt the posture of freely extending forgiveness to others. It's why Jesus taught us to pray, "Forgive us our trespasses as we forgive those who trespass against us." Jesus then appended his own commentary to the Lord's Prayer when he said, "For if you forgive others their trespasses, your heavenly Father will also forgive you, but if you do not forgive others their trespasses, neither will your Father forgive your trespasses." With this in mind, here is a prayer you can pray to help bring your life into the cycle of grace where forgiveness is found and healing abounds.

Lord Jesus Christ, Son of God, have mercy on me a sinner. I confess my own need for forgiveness, for I describe myself justly when I confess I am a sinner. And as a sinner I ask for your mercy and for your forgiveness. Jesus, as you cried from the cross, "Father, forgive them," I ask that you would forgive me. And now as I receive the grace of your free and merciful forgiveness, I make the choice to extend this same grace of forgiveness to those who have sinned against me. I do not justify their actions, but I choose to offer mercy. Jesus, help me to pray concerning those who have wronged me as you prayed concerning those who wronged you—help me to pray, "Father, forgive them." Now, by faith, I receive your forgiveness, Lord Jesus, and in your name I extend forgiveness to those who have sinned against me. Lord Jesus, I seek to belong to the forgiving community of forgiven sinners, and I ask that by your wounds we might all be healed. Amen.

NOTES

Chapter 2—The Story of Simon Wiesenthal

1. Simon Wiesenthal, *The Sunflower* (New York: Schocken, 1997), 14–15.

2. Ibid., 42–43.

3. Ibid., 54.

4. Ibid., 97–98.

Chapter 4—Forgiveness—the Heart of the Christian Gospel

1. Solomon Schimmel, *Wounds Not Healed by Time* (New York: Oxford University Press, 2002), 65.

Chapter 5—Forgiveness—the Cost of Discipleship

1. "Readers Digest." Words and music by Larry Norman. Copyright © 1973 (renewed 2001) GLENWOOD MUSIC CORP. and STRAW BED MUSIC. All rights controlled and administered by GLENWOOD MUSIC CORP. All rights reserved. International copyright secured. Used by permission. *Reprinted by permission of Hal Leonard Corporation.*

Chapter 6—Is Grace More Than Just the Name of a Girl?

1. Dietrich Bonhoeffer, *The Cost of Discipleship* (New York: Touchstone, 1963, 1995), 90.

DON'T JUST READ IT
LIVE IT OUT.

Join the conversation of radical forgiveness on **Facebook, Twitter,** and **Brian Zahnd's blog,** and help start a movement.

WEBSITE:
www.unconditionalthebook.com

TWITTER:
www.twitter.com/brianzahnd
Use the hashtag #unconditional?

FACEBOOK:
www.Facebook.com/unconditionalthebook

BLOG:
www.brianzahnd.com

FREE NEWSLETTERS
TO HELP EMPOWER YOUR LIFE

Why subscribe today?

☐ **DELIVERED DIRECTLY TO YOU.** All you have to do is open your inbox and read.

☐ **EXCLUSIVE CONTENT.** We cover the news overlooked by the mainstream press.

☐ **STAY CURRENT.** Find the latest court rulings, revivals, and cultural trends.

☐ **UPDATE OTHERS.** Easy to forward to friends and family with the click of your mouse.

CHOOSE THE E-NEWSLETTER THAT INTERESTS YOU MOST:

- Christian news
- Daily devotionals
- Spiritual empowerment
- And much, much more

SIGN UP AT: **http://freenewsletters.charismamag.com**